The
Approachability
PLAYBOOK

3 Essential Habits for Thriving Leaders and Teams

Phillip B. Wilson
Founder, Approachable**Leadership**®

VISIT US ONLINE http://ALplaybook.com

Published by Approachable Leadership. Editorial development by Janet Goldstein. Book design by Daniel Hook.

FIRST EDITION

Printed in the United States of America.

ISBN: 0963855441
ISBN-13: 978-0963855442

Praise for *The Approachability Playbook*

The Approachability Playbook is a rare find among those of us who continually work on developing leadership skills in ourselves and in others. Phil Wilson hits the right combination of research insight with practical guidance and exercises to make this read an indispensable part of any leader's skill development toolbox.

    Mark Floyd, Senior Director, Global Labor Relations
    Uber Technologies

If you care about the people who work for you and want to bring out the best in them, read Phil Wilson's *Approachability Playbook*. It is an immensely readable, practical guide to becoming a better boss, and it will make you think and laugh as you turn the pages.

    William Hartman, Director, Employee Relations
    The Boeing Company

Phil...BRAVO! I've been an early adopter and fan of the concept of approachability. The way Phil has so simply illuminated this construct is brilliantly digestible, leaving the reader with a sizable portion of "I can do this." Amongst the sea of leadership approaches, principles, theories, and practices, *The Approachability Playbook* gravitates to the top when it comes to practical actions you can take to get the best out of your workplace interactions and speed with which those changes can be implemented.

    Scott Purvis, Vice President, HR
    Lowe's Home Improvement

There are a lot of studies cited in *The Approachability Playbook*. In an effort to make the book more readable (and approachable), we left notes about sources out of the content.

Are you a nerd like me and interested in reading the studies? Have no fear! If you want to dive into the research behind Approachable Leadership, it's all on our site (we update it regularly as we find more). Simply visit:

http://ApproachableLeadership.com/research

Table of Contents

INTRODUCTION
Are You a Good Boss?

Leadership is hard. Some days—like after helping an employee through a rough patch or watching your team rise to the occasion and reach a big goal—you feel like you've got it nailed. Other days (if you're anything like me) you wonder if you know anything about leadership at all. It can be a struggle.

As the head of a management consulting business I coach, praise, encourage, discipline, listen to, celebrate, and yes, sometimes have to fire, employees. On top of that, many of our consulting clients turn to us for help with their own employee relations issues and leadership crises. These include companies whose employees are in full revolt—the business equivalent of a heart attack or a nasty divorce.

My views about what works (and doesn't work) were learned in the trenches—and it's during the toughest times that you see the best leaders shine. After watching some leaders succeed and others fall flat on their faces, I started asking a question you've probably asked too: *What separates good leaders from those who fail?*

It turns out this question isn't so easy to answer. Many people who seem like they'd be great leaders are actually horrible. And then there are others you underestimate as "not leadership material," only to discover that their people would run into a burning building for them. What often makes the difference is something I call Approachable Leadership.

Approachable Leadership represents a set of day-to-day habits great leaders use to build connection with the people they lead. It's something different from charisma, personality, leadership style, or emotional intelligence. It's a way of engaging that actually forges deeper connections, builds trust, and makes commitment possible. What's more, we've discovered that Approachable Leadership can be learned. It is the best framework I've found to explain what separates the leaders who crumble from the ones who come out of the crucible hard as steel.

Right now this might sound too good to be true. I get it. If you're like me, you're skeptical of books that promise to solve all your leadership issues. This book is different. From Chapter One (where I explain The Connection Model of Approachable Leadership) forward, I think you'll see this isn't a bunch of theory about what *could* work, or what works when things are going great. It isn't some "magic dust" that will make your day-to-day struggles vanish forever. You already know that's not real.

Instead, this is a model based on habits that have been tested and proven by research (you'll see some of this research throughout the book), as well as with real-life leaders in organizations ranging from Fortune 50 global manufacturing and retail operations to small entrepreneurial companies. And in keeping with a model based on habits you can learn, I wanted to share these lessons in a way that will make a difference for people at all levels of leadership and all types of workplaces. Thus the "Playbook."

Think for a minute:

> Are you struggling to connect with someone on your team?
>
> Do some team members avoid you—or are there some people you'd prefer to avoid?
>
> Do you wish your folks made more suggestions or took more initiative?

Chapters Two through Five offer a number of tools or "plays" you can run to improve things.

We've all experienced it when a seemingly great plan doesn't work out. You have to find the one that works for your environment, your people. The same is true with this book. There will be plays that won't work for you or your specific situation. But many of them will. I will also share, throughout the book, a sampling of true stories of good and not-so-good leaders, based on actual situations we've seen in our consulting practice or heard during workshops. I've changed the names because, well, that's the approachable thing to do.

What Makes Approachability Different?

Let me take a guess about you. Since you're the type of person who will pick up and read a book on leadership, my guess is you're already a pretty solid leader. You probably have some great days, a lot of pretty good days, and the occasional day that you wish you hadn't come to work at all. Join the club.

There's a lot of great leadership training out there already. So why doesn't it work all the time? Well, that's a lot like saying, "I know how to swing a golf club, why aren't I a scratch golfer?"

Like the esteemed management thinker Mike Tyson once said:

"Everybody has a plan until they get punched in the mouth."

I've designed this Playbook for a leader like you (and me). Someone who handles things well when they're going good, but could use a crutch, a pointer, or a little coaching when things go into the ditch. Just like that perfect driving range golf swing falls apart when you are a few holes away from your best round ever, great leadership advice tends to fall apart inside the pressure cooker of today's workplace.

The key is to get the habits of approachability right first. It is *the* leadership fundamental.

Before we get started, do you have an idea of how approachable you are? Do you know how well you manage the power balance between colleagues, bosses, and teams? Discover your own "Boss IQ" by completing this simple 12-question quiz. You may be surprised to uncover several opportunities to grow your own approachability. And then start building your Approachable Leadership, one small step and habit at a time.

NOTE: If you aren't a great boss, you probably aren't the best judge of the statements in our quiz. For those who are serious about discovering how others perceive you, we suggest asking someone you trust to take the quiz with your leadership in mind.

⚒ TOOL: The "Good Boss" Quiz

Answer the following questions on a 1 to 5 scale: 1 is "never"; 2 is "not really"; 3 is "sometimes"; 4 is "often"; and 5 is "always."

1. Workers offer "feedback" when they are actually just complaining.
2. I keep an "open-door" policy for employees to meet with me whenever they feel the need.
3. I prefer having workers who can get their jobs done without my support.
4. When an employee approaches my work-area I give them my undivided attention.
5. It takes me a day or two to respond to employees' requests to meet.
6. Employees appear uncomfortable when they discuss difficult matters with me.
7. I am available to meet with employees individually.
8. I am too busy to meet with my workers.
9. It is unrealistic to implement employee ideas.
10. I ask each of my employees what I could change to make their job better.
11. I go out of my way to make employees I supervise feel at ease.
12. Employees I supervise come up with interesting ideas and solutions.

1.	5.	9.
2.	6.	10.
3.	7.	11.
4.	8.	12.

Total Points:

Score Sheet (see below for how to score)

How to score your "Good Boss" quiz:

For each question, look up your answer and then give yourself the designated number of points. When finished, add up all your points for your total approachability score.

Score questions **1**, **3**, **5**, **6**, **8**, and **9** as follows:

Answer	Points
1	5
2	4
3	3
4	2
5	1

On questions **2**, **4**, **7**, **10**, **11**, and **12** score as follows:

Answer	Points
1	1
2	2
3	3
4	4
5	5

If you scored:

54 to 60 – You are **very approachable**.
Congratulations! You are doing a great job. But even the most talented performers have to continue to hone their craft if they want to stay at the top. That's your mission.

48 to 53 – You appear **approachable** to those you lead.
While you are approachable there is still some room to build your leadership skills. This will ensure you don't lose any ground.

42 to 47 – You appear **somewhat approachable**.
There is significant room to build your approachability. Your team's performance (and your performance) will improve if you become more approachable.

36 to 41 – You appear **unapproachable**.
You should start working on your approachability today! Unapproachable leaders suffer much higher turnover, lower productivity and increased work stress than approachable leaders.

35 or less – You appear **very unapproachable**.
This is a real problem, not just for those you lead but for you as well. You need to stop everything you are doing and really work hard to improve your approachability. The silver lining? You will see a lot of

positive changes around you if you just work on this one leadership behavior.

Do you wish you scored a little better? Did you do pretty well, but want to make sure you stay on top? How would other leaders on your team score? After you finish the book check out page 108, where you'll find a link to the free online version of our quiz. You and other leaders on your team will receive complete results (including a breakdown of where you score on the three key areas of **openness**, **understanding** and **support**).

It's important to remember that even the most brilliant plays don't work when the performers lack fundamentals. You have to start with the basics.

Want to be the world's next great pianist? Start with *Chopsticks*. Want to design a skyscraper? Learn to build foundations. Want to be a great leader? Work on your approachability.

Our next chapter lays out the fundamentals of Approachable Leadership.

CHAPTER 1

Leadership That Connects: Mind the Relationship Gap and Build Your Team's Success

> *When the master governs, the people are hardly aware that he exists. Next best is a leader who is loved. Next, one who is feared. The worst is the one who is despised.*
>
> —*Lao Tzu*, Tao Te Ching

Imagine this. You are concentrating on a project, head down, when you look up and notice your boss has appeared without warning.

Or, your phone rings—it hardly ever rings with everyone on email and chat. You're abruptly asked to come down to the VP's office for a quick meeting. You don't know why.

What's your immediate reaction? How do you feel?

What do your own work and life experiences with power tell you? Are there some powerful people in your life you feel more comfortable with than others? How do you usually react when faced with those people and situations? And on the other side, do you sense that some people have a greater challenge asserting themselves to you than others?

The Space Between:
Why All Good Leaders Struggle with Power

People uncomfortable with power will often avoid and defer to powerful people. Those more comfortable around power are easier to spot, as they will be more relaxed and outspoken. Some people and situations allow us to feel more open to power, and others make us want to avoid it.

The space between these two poles is called "power distance." The idea of power distance was first introduced by Professor Geert Hofstede in his 1980 book *Culture's Consequences*. Hofstede studied how over 100,000 folks from dozens of different cultures dealt with people in power, and found that different cultures differ in their relationship to power. Some cultures had wide "power distance," or were very deferential to power, while others were less so.

Beyond Hofstede's focus on how different cultures deal with power, there are also several other causes of power distance. It may come from our early experiences with powerful people like parents, teachers, clergy, doctors, coaches, and other leaders. Or it could be influenced by factors like culture, race, gender, wealth, and health.

Each of us has a different relationship to power. Someone's power distance with you may be based on prior experiences with you, or it may be largely based on earlier experiences with powerful people.

Power distance isn't always bad. Deferring to your parent, teacher, coach, or boss is sometimes the right move. But many times power distance causes problems. Fear of leaders and those of higher rank or status—whether "real" or imagined—causes disengagement, turnover, low innovation, workplace stress, and other concerns like serious miscommunications, even in life-and-death situations.

Power distance may be narrow or wide. Regardless, the most effective leaders keep this power distance gap as small as possible. As I like to say, they "mind the gap."

When we look at what this means for us individually, we can begin to observe how we respond to others and how people respond to us. You can think about ways to make it safe and comfortable for staff and peers to raise questions, make suggestions, give you feedback, confront you with a problem, or just get something off their chest. If you're not creating this sort of environment, then you are missing out on a lot of opportunities.

It's hard not to be skeptical though, especially when we think about the people who push our buttons the most. At a recent training workshop, Pam, a quality supervisor, said to me after the session was over, "I'd really like to believe this will work, but I've got a guy who I've had a bad relationship with for seventeen years. We fight at least once a week over a stupid production report that should take five minutes to complete, but with complaining takes more than twenty minutes because he hates it so much. No way he's going to change."

"You may be right, Pam," I said. "But what do you have to lose? Why don't you give it a try?" We strategized briefly and she went to talk to him. The next day she slipped in just as the training session for another group was ending.

"Well, I owe you an apology. It worked," she smiled. "I told him what we talked about—that I was frustrated that we always battled over the form and I asked what he thought could make it better. He made a small suggestion that will save us some time each week and then we had the best conversation we've ever had. It was like he was a different person."

"How much will it save?" I asked.

"About 15 minutes a week for each of us, not to mention all the stress these confrontations have caused me over the years."

When you add up the all-in costs that one minor change might save the company, it could come to thousands of dollars a year. Not only that, Pam goes home a *lot* happier.

Making others comfortable around you isn't just some "feel-good" trick. It can have major impacts on your business and make your job a lot easier, too, just like it did for Pam. You never know which conversation will result in saving you an operational headache, fix a quality problem that's been causing added expenses, enhance communication and collaboration, or save a key customer relationship.

The very first hurdle in achieving any of these incremental changes is minimizing the aversion many people have to approaching someone in power. No matter how open you are to being a great boss and creating a culture of openness, you can't just start running around hounding people to talk to you. They must want to come to you. So how do you build connection without making people suspicious of your motives or authenticity? How do you calm these fears and put people at ease?

In order to answer these questions, we must first try to understand people's relationships with power.

Paleo Leadership: How Fear and Power Get in Our Way

We humans like to think we are pretty advanced. After all, we live in the most technologically innovative society in the history of mankind. Developments continue to come at a mind-boggling rate. We are healthier, wealthier, and more connected than ever before.

However, if you take the long view, humans today aren't much different from our ancestors of 10,000 years ago. British comedian David Allen explains the problem this way:

When we're at work and the boss approaches, our flight-or-fight reflexes immediately kick in. Our blood pressure rises and adrenaline pumps through our bodies. Then, when we're already jacked up, the boss has the nerve to ask us a question or—gasp—call us by our last name.

This, Allen observes, is when our bodies go into overdrive.

Allen laments that if we could just act like we did in caveman times, things wouldn't be so hard on our bodies. Rather than bursting a blood vessel, we would simply pick up a chair and bash our boss over the head with it. But, seeing as that's not allowed in modern society, we instead take the abuse and deal with it internally.

This approach has all kinds of negative consequences. It creates disease and depression. We then take it out on our co-workers. On our way home we take it out on innocent pedestrians (admit it—you've flipped someone the bird you really meant for your boss). Then, when we get home, our families bear the brunt of our bad day.

Allen's story may be amusing, but it also teaches an important leadership lesson. As leaders, we don't envision ourselves as saber-tooth tigers on the savannah. But at a primal level—especially as the power distance gap grows—that's *exactly* how we, as leaders and bosses, are experienced. If our relationships aren't great, we trigger those same flight-or-fight stressors ourselves. And it's how we experience *our* leaders and bosses.

There's a lot of chaos and drama lurking under the surface of our work relationships, and that chaos is interfering with the real work that needs to get done and the real conversations that need to take place.

Lessons in Leadership: Approachability and Deming's 14 Points of Management

W. Edwards Deming is considered the most important management thinker of the twentieth century. His work inspired the Toyota Production System, the quality movement, Six Sigma, and lean manufacturing. His focus on efficiency and quality sometimes make people think Deming cared more about systems and less about relationships. However, one of the surprising things about Deming's work is how much of it relates to leadership. For example, look at Deming's 14 Points of Management:

1. Constancy of purpose to improve
2. Adopt the philosophy
3. End mass inspections
4. Don't award business on price alone
5. Constantly improve the system of production and service
6. Institute training
7. Adopt and institute leadership
8. Drive out fear
9. Break down barriers between staff
10. Eliminate slogans and targets for the workforce
11. Eliminate numerical quotas
12. Remove barriers that rob people of pride in workmanship

13. Encourage education and self-improvement
14. Take action to accomplish the transformation

In this list are multiple references to leadership versus management. Two that stand out are points 8 and 9. But items 3 and 10-12 are also directly related to eliminating fear-based management. Nearly half of Deming's list of key principles deals directly with reducing fear—shrinking the gap—in the workplace.

Don't Speak Korean in the Cockpit: Shrinking Power Distance Helps Avoid Disasters

Quick quiz. Who had the worst airline safety record from 1985 to 1999?
   a) Malaysia Airlines
   b) Delta Airlines
   c) Lufthansa
   d) Korean Air Lines

Korean Air Lines (KAL), today considered one of the premier airlines in the world, was the most dangerous major airline in the 1990s. They had more than *twice* as many incidents per flight kilometer as U.S. airlines during the same period. From 1983 to 1999 KAL suffered over a dozen near misses and nearly 700 fatalities in 6 separate plane crashes.

In one tragic incident, a KAL Boeing 747 mistakenly flew into restricted Soviet airspace—where it was quickly blown out of the sky, killing all 269 people on board. Another 206 passengers died in 1997 when KAL Flight 801 flew right into the side of Nimitz Hill in Guam. As a result, Delta and Air France both suspended their flying partnerships with KAL and the U.S. military would not allow U.S. troops to travel on KAL flights.

Korean Airlines hasn't had a fatal accident since 1999. That's because in 2000, KAL hired David Greenberg, a former Delta Airlines flight operations executive (and, significantly, an American) to turn their safety problems around.

Greenberg decided that drastic measures were needed. And perhaps none was more important—or controversial—than this: He required all pilots at KAL to stop speaking Korean and only speak English in the cockpit.

Why?

Malcolm Gladwell tells the story of this amazing turnaround in his book *Outliers: The Story of Success*. He starts by pointing to Professor Geert Hofstede's work on power distance.

He learned from Hofstede's focus on world cultures that Asian and Latin cultures have a high deference to hierarchy and authority and therefore a wider power distance. Cultures like those in the United States and Europe have lower deference for authority and hierarchy and therefore a smaller power distance. These findings have remained consistent for over 30 years (most recently in follow-up research by Hofstede in 2010).

Hofstede's Power Distance Index

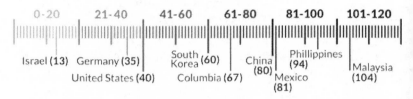

| 0-20 | 21-40 | 41-60 | 61-80 | 81-100 | 101-120 |

Israel (13)   Germany (35)
United States (40)

South Korea (60)
Columbia (67)

China (80)

Phillippines (94)
Mexico (81)

Malaysia (104)

Hofstede found each culture's different relationship to power showed up in varied and sometimes surprising ways. One of the most common indicators of the degree of power distance in a culture is language. The more power distance, the more deference is paid to authority figures through language. This is one reason why Greenberg decided to change the language in KAL cockpits. As the power distance gap widens, the language is less likely to include the words to confront more powerful people.

Gladwell focuses on this in his detailed analysis of what happened during the KAL Flight 801 crash in Guam. Flight 801 reached Guam in the middle of a furious thunderstorm with very low physical visibility. The captain, who was overtired and unfocused, chose to land the plane on a "visual approach"—that is, without the aid of radar. This was a fatal decision, one Gladwell claims was noticed by the rest of the flight crew but was ineffectively—and, in Korean, perhaps impossibly—communicated. He blames power distance.

The flight crew used what is called "mitigated speech" in their attempt to warn the Captain that trying to land without the radar would be suicide. Rather than saying,

*"Captain, it is a dangerous mistake to try
to make a visual approach in this rain."*

They said,

"Captain, the weather radar has helped us a lot."

Or,

"Don't you think it rains more?"

Mitigated speech is a signal.

It indicates someone disagrees with a course of action, but is also trying to be polite. It means there's a power distance gap.

For most leaders, ignoring this signal only causes us to miss an opportunity to connect or hear a new idea. But in some cases—like that night on KAL flight 801, or in a workplace where employees work with heavy equipment, chemicals, or harnesses—ignoring mitigated speech can be a matter of life or death.

This whole idea of changing the language to change the culture is compelling, isn't it? Unfortunately, shrinking the power distance gap is not always that simple. After all, there are plenty of examples of plane crashes where the flight crew spoke English.

The problem of communication gaps isn't just cultural. There are countless reasons why someone might feel uncomfortable confronting their boss, even in a life or death situation. That's why leader approachability is such a critical behavior—it's about connection, not just communication. No matter what the causes of a power distance gap, approachability is the only way to effectively shrink it.

So how do you become more approachable? First, you can use a simple tool to assess the gaps in any relationship you have or are concerned about, and then you can begin to apply specific action steps to increase your approachability (or to bridge the gap with someone you find unapproachable).

 ## TOOL: Recognizing Approachability Gaps

Power distance gaps cause major problems. But how do you tell if there is a gap? This tool helps you recognize behavior that suggests a power distance problem.

There are three places where the gap might show up: (1) physical gaps, (2) verbal gaps, and (3) behavioral gaps (between what someone says and what they do). Use the assessment below to recognize signals of power distance. When you notice one, use the discussion starters to help shrink the gap.

Physical Gaps

If someone is experiencing power distance it will often show up in their physical behavior. They will try to avoid the more powerful person.

- Physical distance, turned toward an "exit"
- Avoiding eye contact, looking at ceiling or floor
- Closed body language (arms crossed)
- Distracted, seems lost in thought
- Holding back or agitated body language

Verbal Gaps

These are the most common signals you will notice. Indirect or mitigated speech often expresses power distance.

Watch for mitigated speech like:
- Hints ("I wonder if...")
- Preference ("perhaps we should...")
- Question ("do you think ___ would work?"), or
- Team suggestion ("why don't we try ___?")
- Look for attempts to "sugarcoat" or downplay bad news
- Being overly polite or deferential
- Quickly deferring or backing down when rejected by someone in power

Behavioral Gaps

Many times actions speak louder than words. Watch for gaps between what someone says and what they do.

- Promising one thing, doing another
- No follow-through or follow-up

- Passive-aggressive actions
- Being "too busy" or procrastinating
- "Changing mind" about importance of issue

Discussion Starters
When you notice specific gaps, use the following discussion starters to help shrink the gap.
- "You seem uncomfortable. It's OK—I really want to know what you think."
- "I'm not 100% sure what I think about this myself. Tell me what you really think."
- "OK, that's what I do [name behavior] when I'm not sure if I should say something. What's up?"
- "I need your help. Can you be honest and tell me exactly what you think about this?"
- "I may be completely off base here, I don't know. Can you tell me what you really think?"

*You can download all the tools mentioned in the book at http://ALplaybook.com

The Connection Model:
The Three Pillars of Approachable Leadership

Are you likely to succeed as a leader? The best way to tell is to look at your relationships. Leadership starts with connection. Approachable leaders stand out through the connections they share with the people they lead. They engage in daily habits that build up (rather than erode) connection.

The Connection Model describes how leaders can use approachable behavior to build connection with coworkers. Here's how we define Approachable Leadership:

Approachable leaders connect with others by being *Open, Understanding, and Supportive*

These behaviors form the three pillars of Approachable Leadership.

The Connection Model

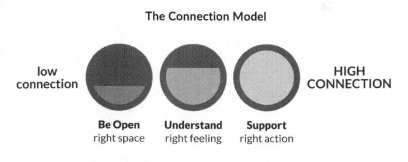

low connection   HIGH CONNECTION

Be Open
right space

Understand
right feeling

Support
right action

Each of these behaviors can be expressed through habits that can be learned and practiced every day. Approachable Leaders show:
- *Openness* by being available, welcoming, and inviting—creating and maintaining "Right Space."
- *Understanding* through warmth, active listening, and empathy—exhibiting "Right Feeling."
- *Support* by being receptive to others, then following up and following through—performing "Right Action."

The next three chapters fully explain each of these pillars and provide practical tools to help you start using the habits in your daily leadership. These habits are not magic, nor do they require you to change your personality or transform into an off-the-charts charismatic leader.

Instead you'll learn a few simple and specific skills that you can readily apply with your own team to shrink power distance, reduce fear, and build stronger connections.

Are you ready to start?

YOUR TURN ▶ Think about examples in your own life where you have dealt with a power distance gap. Maybe there were times when:

- You personally had to come up with the courage to tell someone more powerful than you something that you were reluctant to tell them?
- You didn't tell somebody in a more powerful position something that you later wished you had?
- Someone with low power had the courage to tell you something that they were reluctant to share?
- Someone failed to tell you something important because they were in a less powerful position?

Name three ways you might shrink the power distance gap between yourself and a person you lead:

1.

2.

3.

Name three ways you might shrink the power distance gap between yourself and someone higher up than you in the organization, or a peer where you perceive/experience a strong power gap:

1.

2.

3.

Review the *Recognizing Gaps Tool* (page 28) before your next one-on-one meeting. Do you notice any power distance signals?

CHAPTER 2

The "Curb Appeal" Factor: Openness and "Right Space"

> " *It's really easy to have a nice philosophy about openness, but moving the world in that direction is* " *a different thing. It requires both understanding where you want to go and being pragmatic about getting there.*

—Mark Zuckerberg

The root for the word approach means "To draw near or to neighbor." Leaders should try to embrace what it means to be neighborly.

Are you a good neighbor to your employees? What do you do to draw people to you? Do you put out the welcome mat? Do you have curb appeal?

If you've watched any HGTV, you know how important "curb appeal" is to a house. A house with curb appeal is inviting. It may have an attractive walkway leading to the front door, flowers that draw the eye, a porch that says, "We're ready for you." People can't wait to go in. The house with curb appeal sells for top dollar. The house with no curb appeal stays on the market for months and sells below market.

What's Your Curb Appeal?

A big-box hardware store chain recently did a training video for its managers. In the video, a manager walks around the store talking to everyone. Everywhere he goes, right in front of him, is a metaphoric "welcome mat." Welcome mats are neighborly. They increase curb appeal.

Imagine we all have welcome mats that slide along the floor in front of us as we go about our day. Is your mat inviting? Or does it say something like this?

The "unwelcome mat" of the unapproachable boss.

The first step to being an approachable leader? Create what I call the "Right Space." This means being available, open and welcoming to others. Creating the feeling of, "Hey, great to see you. Come on in." Your welcome mat is out.

A lot of managers think they get this right simply because they have an "open door" policy. No question that a door that's always closed is unapproachable. But being welcoming isn't just about physical availability. It is more about how you act when somebody walks through that open door.

Inviting someone in and then continuing to type away on your computer isn't going to cut it. Neither is saying you're listening and then picking up your phone the moment you get a text, email, or phone call. Do this and people feel like you don't value them or what they have to say.

If you truly want others to approach you, pay attention to your non-verbal behavior. What signals do you send to tell others you are available and happy to see them? Do you have a welcome mat or an unwelcome mat in front of you as you walk through your day as a leader? What does it say about you most of the time? What would you like it to say?

I know it sounds cliché, but your grandma was right—nothing is more inviting or more approachable than a smile.

A 2014 study published by the National Academy of Sciences actually confirms this. The study looked at 65 different facial features to determine what features gave people the first impression of approachability, attractiveness, or dominance. By very briefly showing people images of these different expressions, researchers confirmed that the most important factor related to approachability was a smile. Smiling was associated with approachability 96.5% of the time—more than even attractiveness. Smiling was also *negatively* associated with dominance (we will soon learn why that is very important for leaders).

Blind Spots, Hidden Areas and Open Windows

The challenge we face when we want to become more welcoming is that we're often not aware of the messages (the smiles, scowls, looks of boredom, lack of eye contact) we're sending out over the course of the average workday.

After 20 years dealing with some of the toughest situations with bosses and teams, I've heard just about everything. But at a recent workshop where we were exploring the idea of Right Space, an attendee named Karen shared a story about a blind spot she discovered and her own "unwelcome mat." It caught me so off guard that I had to look it up!

She told the class about a day her coworker revealed a blind spot to her. He told her she suffers from a condition known as RBF or "resting bitch face."

Seriously, it's a thing. And guys, you're not immune—just look at Kanye West. In fact, a 2016 study by behavioral researchers Jason Rogers and Abbe Macbeth at Noldus Information Technology analyzed "neutral" facial expressions with celebrity "RBF" expressions and found that a subtle sign of contempt was the defining factor in people's negative reactions, and it was found equally in male and female faces.

Luckily, Karen is generally friendly and approachable and a coworker let her know. She's worked on her facial expression ever since. No surprise, but she's seen a real change in the way coworkers engage with her. She also got a promotion that had been delayed longer than she expected. Coincidence? I doubt it.

Leaders who struggle with curb appeal and connecting with their teams often figure out a couple of quick ways to improve when they learn a few specific steps they can take to assess—and then shift—their perceived openness. It's about slowly building connections with others by sharing with them and taking the brave step of asking for more feedback.

One of the favorite tools from our Approachable Leadership Workshop is *The Approachability Window.*

As the name suggests, this is a visual tool and prompt to help leaders "open the window" on who they are and how they are perceived. When our workshop participants explore their approachability windows, many of them realize that their office "door" might be open, but their approachability window is closed. The space around them is stuffy and no one wants to come near.

Then you have others who fling their personal window open so wide that the gusts of wind (e.g., over-sharing, hot air, directives) leave no calm space for anyone to breathe (these are the people who never really grasped the concept of boundaries). Both habits ultimately increase distance between leaders and those they lead.

A key part of increasing our approachability is improving our self-awareness. *The Approachability Window* is designed to do just that.

TOOL: The Approachability Window

This tool helps you improve relationships by revealing more about yourself and seeking feedback. When you don't seek feedback, you create blind spots. When you don't share with others, you close them out and withdraw. When people feel they know you, they experience a smaller power distance gap.

The Approachability Window helps you visualize areas where you're an "open book"; areas you keep hidden from others; and areas where you have blind spots. Part of being approachable and growing relationships with others is opening your Approachability Window by sharing from *your* hidden areas and learning about your blind spots.

Approachability Window

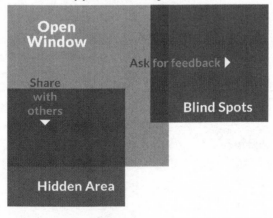

What the "Windows" Mean

If you look at the diagram above, you see that there are three different boxes. The top-left box is the "open" window, the area of feelings, beliefs, and experiences you have shared (or are willing to share) with others. This area includes the things everybody knows about you—things they can easily observe or that you would share with a stranger without thinking too much about it. It also includes the things that you disclose to others over time as you grow a connection with them.

The top right area is made up of your blind spots. The only way these are revealed to you is by somebody else telling you. They can be as minor as, "You have spinach in your teeth" to major revelations like, "You suffer from RBF."

The bottom left box is the "hidden" area. These are things that are known by you but unknown by others. This is a very important part of the Approachability Window. As you grow relationships with others, you begin to reveal things that they don't know. As a relationship grows stronger and stronger, you'll reveal more and more about yourself, in effect opening your Approachability Window wider and wider.

Using the Tool:
Sharing Yourself and Requesting Feedback

It's important to remember that this as an exchange. You're not unloading a dump truck. Instead, you grow relationships slowly, over time.

It should play out like this: Offer something from your hidden area. If the other individual reveals something to you from their hidden area, your original offer to grow the relationship is accepted. Once that exchange has been made, then you can offer something else from your hidden area at another time.

Think about the Approachability Window as a way to create an open space for others. You create that welcoming space by being open and relaxed and sharing with others in your open area. The more you can reveal of yourself, the more comfortable others will be around you and the more likely it is that you'll find areas in common. This is just good conversation. It breaks down barriers and lets others know it is safe to share with you.

Last, but not least, make sure that you also let people know you are open to and welcome feedback. This is the only way you learn about your blind spots.

Tips to Encourage Feedback
- Sincerely ask for input.
- Stop/Start. What should I start doing? What should I stop doing?
- Stress the value of feedback. Why is it important? Why is this person uniquely able to provide it?
- LISTEN! Use our *Active Listening Tool* (page 61) to make sure you do a good job of listening. This by itself encourages feedback.
- Don't be defensive! Accept the feedback, be open-minded and reflect on it. *Thank them—it's a gift!*

Tips to Grow Relationships with the Approachability Window
- Take your time–sharing too much too soon can be worse than not sharing. Go slow.
- Ask questions. Don't interrogate but show interest and learn as much as you can.
- When you share with someone mention the relationship—"I don't tell everyone this, but we are close so I'll tell you..."
- Be empathetic (don't one-up, offer unsolicited advice, etc.) Use our *Empathy Toolkit*.
- Don't share secrets.
- Acknowledge and appreciate if they reveal something new.

NOTE: The Approachability Window is based heavily on the Johari Window developed by Joseph Luft and Harrington Ingram in 1955. If you'd like to learn more about this powerful interpersonal development tool the Wikipedia page on Johari Window is a great place to start.

Lessons in Leadership: When Blind Spots Lead to Managing from On High

There's this guy, we'll call him Frank. Frank came to one of our workshops and shared a story. He had just started a new job as supervisor of an operation that he didn't have much experience with. The first few weeks on the job, Frank spent quite a bit of time standing above the assembly operation trying to get a good view so he could better understand how the whole process worked.

When Frank was up there by himself, he typically stood with his arms crossed and, as you can imagine, no real expression on his face. However, these qualities completely changed when someone popped over to ask him a question. Frank was naturally very animated when he spoke, always making faces and waving his arms.

After about two weeks of this scene playing out over and over again above his crew, one brave employee went up to the perch and gave him some feedback. He asked Frank what he'd been doing up there for the last week or two. Frank told him.

The brave employee said, "Okay, well look at it from our point of view. You stand up here with your arms crossed and watch us for hours. Then you get really fired up when someone comes to talk to you. A lot of the guys on the floor think that you are watching what everybody's doing and then complaining about how they're doing it. They think you're trying to figure out who you can fire."

Frank was astounded. He felt like he'd been trying to be a great leader by watching his team in order to really understanding how things worked. He had no idea that he was creating such negative feelings among the people that he was leading. If he had not received that feedback, he may never have thought about his own non-verbal behavior and how it was impacting others around him.

That exchange itself took a lot of courage. It also showed a combination of things. First, the employee wasn't afraid to bridge the gap between the leader and himself. That could be because of a prior history of sharing that sort of information with leaders who took it well. Or it could be he was so frustrated he didn't care. Maybe he just drew the short straw and it was his turn to go onto the firing line.

Whatever happened, luckily this leader was open to the feedback. It gave Frank the opportunity to change his behavior. It also gave him a chance to create understanding with his co-workers about what he was doing while he was observing them.

The good news is that Frank formed a great relationship both with the employee who gave him the initial feedback and also with the co-workers on the line. This *story became a way for everyone to connect. And it also obviously was a high impact moment in his own career.*

By the time I heard Frank tell that story, he was a top level manager at one of the most respected companies in the world. Today, Frank is a great example of an approachable leader.

Flight or Fight...or Food

Our flight or fight instincts are innate. They happen outside our control. Even people we like (or love—like a parent, spouse, or child) can create feelings of "flight or fight" as they come near.

Imagine a growling wolf creeping at you through the trees.

Now think about a baby deer frolicking in circles looking for acorns.

For the most part, we all have the same reactions to those two things. We see a wolf and we fly right on out of those woods. But we see a deer, and we find ourselves a nice little tree to sit under and enjoy the moment.

However, one study found some very interesting reactions to the deer and the wolf. The researchers took images like these (as well as another, more neutral image) and had people look at them. Once the subject was fixated on the image, the researchers started moving it closer and closer to them. What they found was that no matter what the image was, the reaction was the same—get out of the way.

The flight or fight reaction is triggered in the most primitive part of our brain. And it goes off even if the person or the engagement that's approaching is somebody we like or an event we want to go to! Think about being approached by your own spouse or child. At times, this can create feelings of dread, even if it's just to give you a kiss on the cheek. What about a fast approaching vacation? This can most certainly cause stress, even if you've wanted to visit this place your whole life.

So what do you do?

If you can't approach people without triggering their primal urge to run away or hit you with a blunt object, what can you do?

Make yourself available for others to approach you.

This means creating time and space when you are clearly available and encouraging people to come by and visit with you. Bribe them if you have to. Food works great. Haven't you ever popped by someone's work area just to get some candy? Games work too (fantasy football is the big one around our office). Anything that creates an excuse for someone to approach you reverses approach aversion.

I realize this isn't always easy to do, especially in today's workplace when we are asked to do more with less. Spans of control are expanding to the breaking point.

While technology certainly makes things easier, it also creates a lot of distractions and the expectation that we should "always be on" and available to others. It's hard to connect with others in the real world if we spend 99% of our time on conference calls and webinars in the virtual world.

That's why as leaders we must not only create, but protect the time we set aside for what's important in our lives. This includes time for people to connect with us. Whether that is scheduling one-on-one meetings, coffee or lunch, or having a clear "office hour" period, we have to commit to providing this time and space for others to approach us.

 ## TOOL: The Elements of Right Space

Approachable Leadership begins with being welcoming and creating the Right Space. This tool provides practical tips on how to be available, warm, and present. Use the tool to identify opportunities to improve your physical space, your behavior, your availability, and your presence.

Physical Space
- Is the physical space inviting and warm?
- Is there a comfortable place to sit?
- Have you cleared any obstacles between you (same side of desk)?
- Are there personal objects or discussion starters?
- Is it quiet? Can it be private?

- Is there a reason to visit? Food works great—so do games.

Behavior
- Are you welcoming and neighborly?
- Are you smiling? Remember that you smile with your mouth and eyes.
- Have you asked open-ended questions?
- Are you doing more than half the talking? Shut up.
- How are they feeling? Are they comfortable?
- Are you observing and asking what they need?

Availability
- Are you available to meet when needed?
- Do you block scheduled "drop in" time?
- Is there a convenient way to schedule time on your calendar?
- Do you allow interruptions for emergency situations?
- Do you "advertise" ways to meet with you?

Presence
- Full stop. Give your full attention.
- Put away your phone, close your laptop. No distractions.
- Close your door or signal to others that you are in a meeting.
- Listen actively. Don't try to think of what you'll say next.

- Summarize what you've heard and confirm understanding.
- Refrain from problem-solving until you are asked.

Lessons in Leadership: Joe Breaks in the New Supervisor

"OK, watch this," Joe whispers to Bob, another grizzled veteran. "The kid's about to drop a 'Because I'm the boss' on me." Kyle, the new supervisor, walks up to Joe.

"Hey, Joe," Kyle says in the most cheerful tone he can muster.

"Hey," Joe replies abruptly without looking up.

"I noticed you aren't pulling that part the way we talked about yesterday," Kyle notes gingerly, "What's up?"

"Yeah, I tried that Kyle," Joe retorts. "Like I told you yesterday, it doesn't work. So I went ahead and switched back to doing it the way that has worked since before you were able to wipe your own tail."

"Look Joe, it isn't going to be quicker right off the bat, but it really looks like this new way is about ten percent more efficient," Kyle pleads. "Can you just try a little longer?"

"Kyle, it's not more efficient. I know it's not. I also know you don't know what you're talking about. So why should I waste a bunch of time trying something I know doesn't work?"

Kyle's face is blotched red as he searches for his next words. "Because I asked you to and I'm the boss," he says.

"Kyle, I like you and I think you're going to be a fine supervisor one day. But I'm not pulling the part any different than I have the last 22 years. You can write me up or whatever you need to do, but I'm not doing it because it's a waste of time and it's stupid."

Kyle walks away dejected. Joe fist bumps Bob with a smile.

Watching a new supervisor learn the ropes can be painful. Joe and Bob also know it can be a little bit entertaining (for everyone but the new supervisor). Joe and Bob know something about power that Kyle has yet to learn.

Let's return to Joe for a second. He didn't decide to give Kyle a hard time out of the blue. Kyle was new. Why did Joe want to haze his new supervisor? His reaction was based on fear. And that fear didn't just appear out of nowhere.

Joe has worked at the company a long time. He's seen a succession of leaders over the years. Some of those *leaders were pretty good, but most of them weren't. Joe has felt threatened and scared about his job (and his ability to provide for his family) on many occasions during his career. There were times when he wished he could move to a different company, but felt stuck and helpless. He was scared to start over.*

There was one time, though, when Joe almost did quit. It would have been devastating to his career and his family. But his boss—who he and his buddies still refer to as "The Jerk"—took pleasure in making him and his coworkers feel afraid. Every day, coming to work was awful. Joe felt like he was on the savannah and The Jerk was a saber-tooth tiger.

Every time The Jerk approached, Joe's heart sank, his body clinched, and he prepared for the worst. The day The Jerk left due to a promotion (he was not fired, of course), was one of the happiest in Joe's life. Literally—right up there with his marriage and the birth of his two kids.

Joe thinks about The Jerk almost every time he walks into work; even today, 11 years after The Jerk left. He thinks about him on his drive to work. He thinks about him when he walks by his old office (which Joe passes every time he goes to the bathroom—and every time he remembers how he used to walk out of his way to use the bathrooms on the other side of the plant just to avoid his old boss). Joe knows he was one of the lucky ones. A lot of guys—good guys—got fired in those days.

How do your employees view you as a leader? We don't often dwell on that. But many of the people you lead believe you hold their whole livelihood in your hands. That might feel wrong (it might even be wrong), but that is how they perceive the world. It impacts how they view everything you do and say.

This reality may seem weird to a first-level leader, especially a new one. You may not feel you have much power. You may be living in fear yourself about what's coming around the next corner. You don't understand how anyone can see you as a threat. But you are, and your behavior impacts those around you. Imagine yourself as that saber-tooth tiger. How might you behave differently as you wander the savannah of your work?

Approach aversion is a valuable lesson. Many of your employees see you as a friend, but still are concerned when you approach. Others see you as the saber-tooth tiger. As you think about your leadership, think about how others react to your approach. Their reaction may seem irrational (at least from your point of view) or completely unwarranted. However, you don't get to choose how others react to you. All you can control is the space you create around you.

You take your followers as they come. Create the Right Space, where they feel safe and secure approaching you.

Reaching the "Retreaters": Sometimes You Need to Walk Around and Knock on Doors

Now that I have you scared to leave your desk, it's time to reverse field. Some people aren't going to approach you. Their power distance is so wide they'll be like Joe and walk to the other side of the building to avoid seeing you. It may have nothing to do with anything you've ever done. But in the end that doesn't matter.

You have no choice. You have to go to them. This is what I call LBWA or "Leading by Walking Around" (coined "managing by wandering around" at HP during the 1970s). However, since these are the individuals most worried about people in power positions, the ones with the highest level of approach aversion, you have to handle these encounters with care.

Here are some tips on how to approach someone who may be avoiding you because of power distance:

1. **Go slow**. Remember, power distance may cause them a lot of anxiety. So take it easy and try to build the relationship one small step at a time.
2. **Be available**. Make it a point to walk by and say hello every once in a while. Smile (and remember to smile with your mouth *and* your eyes).
3. **Start shallow, then deep**. Go back and look at the *Approachability Window Tool*. Remember to begin growing the relationship by sharing from your open area (sports, the weather, what's going on in town).

Obviously, also look for work-related reasons to interact. Find areas of common interest. As the comfort level improves, begin to share more from your Hidden area. Remember, it is about offer and acceptance, and someone with a power distance gap may take quite a while to accept your offer.

4. **Don't get discouraged**. If you're making an effort, you are making progress (even if it may seem like you are treading water). Keep going.

5. **Let others know you want to grow the relationship**. If this individual is close with someone else at work, you may try to build a relationship with that other person. They might help, and this will further signal that you truly care about your relationships with employees. Always be aware of the creep factor, though. Creepers aren't approachable at all.

6. **Use the *Elements of Right Space Tool***. While this tool is primarily geared to making your own work area more welcoming, you can apply a lot of the same principles as you begin your LBWA trips.

You may not be able to connect with everyone you lead. Nonetheless, you should try. Never let the fact that someone has an aversion to people in power stop you from growing the relationship. The stakes are too high—for you, your coworker, and your business.

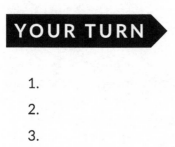

YOUR TURN

What can you do to make your work area more welcoming and inviting?

1.

2.

3.

Commit to make at least one change in each of the four key areas: physical space, availability, warmth and presence. Use the *Elements of Right Space Tool* for ideas.

Additionally, consider making a point each week to schedule one meeting in the office of the person you need to talk to (rather than having him come to your office). This is a nice, easy way to take some of the hierarchy out of day to day interactions.

Should you choose to incorporate this into your leadership practice, consider also giving yourself an additional 10 minutes to "work the room" on your way to the meeting. The more you make your appearance in different departments a part of the norm, the less it will be seen as a cause for conversation, or worse, for alarm.

Can you think of a coworker who has a high power distance relationship? How would you use the *Approachability Window Tool* to bridge that gap?

What opportunities or dangers could you miss if your employees felt uncomfortable approaching you?

CHAPTER 3

The Good Neighbor:
Understanding and "Right Feeling"

 *I love the Lord, because He hears my
voice...
Because He bends down to listen*

—Psalm 116:1-2, NLT

Did you know you can get naked with other people while keeping your clothes on? I do it every month.

Confused? *Getting naked* means becoming vulnerable and sharing with others in a deep way. I keep a regular date with a small group of friends once a month where we do just that.

Seeking Connection:
Getting Naked (with Your Clothes On)

We talk about life stuff. Our kids. Our spouses. Work. Goals and dreams. Failures. Things that make us really happy. Things that make us sad. You know, all the stuff that make us human.

Do you belong to any groups like that? Maybe a church community or accountability group? A support group? Some old friends you fish or hike with? The crew at the gym? These can be some of the most important relationships in

---

our lives. If you don't have a group like this, you should find one.

I belong to something called a forum, as part of a worldwide group called Entrepreneur's Organization (EO). There are over 11,000 entrepreneur members of EO. My forum is a group of eight local members.

When I first joined EO I thought it would be a cool way to connect with other entrepreneurs. What I didn't expect was how profoundly it would impact my life.

The first time I met up with these guys one of them told me it was like Alcoholics Anonymous for entrepreneurs. I thought that was weird.

I've seen how AA helps people. I've watched it work in the lives of some really close friends. To think that I needed a meeting like that in my life wasn't something I was comfortable with at the time. After all, I was a successful guy. I just wanted to talk to some fellow business owners about what worked and what didn't work in their businesses.

Boy, was I wrong.

Before I could start going to forum meetings I was required to go to a class where I learned the EO forum basics. Really. Even though I spend a lot of time facilitating tough discussions with others, I was surprised at how much I still had to learn. There are two key elements to all forum meetings that, as luck would have it, are also essential to approachable leaders. The two elements are confidentiality and a "Gestalt" mindset.

Confidentiality. Forum has to be a safe place for people to share intimate details of their life. Remember the *Approachability Window* (see page 40)? In the open window are things we all feel comfortable sharing with others, even total strangers. Then there are things that we might share with someone as we get closer to them. This is our hidden area.

In our forum meetings we commit to focusing on the far margins of our hidden area—what we call the "5% areas" of life. Those 5% areas are at both ends of the spectrum: your happiest moments and your saddest ones. Think about it like this:

The 5% Areas

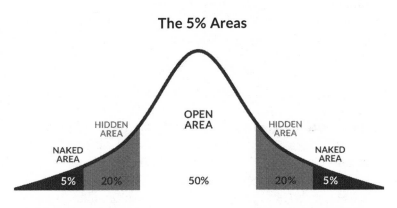

Saddest, negative experiences and feelings

Happiest, positive experiences and feelings

Your 5% areas are things you might only share with your closest relatives or friends. However, there may be things in these areas you don't even want to share with relatives or friends. Your happiest 5% might feel like bragging or create feelings of jealousy. Your saddest 5% might be embarrassing or cause pain. But holding these things inside isn't great for you either. That's where a group like the forum can be so valuable.

For someone to feel comfortable sharing things in their top and bottom 5% it has to be 100% confidential. This is so important we discuss it before every forum meeting. If there is even the slightest breach of confidentiality, that person is kicked out of the forum forever.

Gestalt mindset. The second key element of forum is called the Gestalt mindset. The big idea of the Gestalt mindset is the assumption that people are completely capable of handling their own lives. The purpose of a Gestalt discussion, therefore, is not to "fix" the person. Instead, we try to help them fully understand their own experiences and emotions so they feel ready to handle things themselves.

In forum meetings we hold Gestalt discussions. Someone starts by presenting a current situation they're facing. The rest of us listen. One member is assigned to "coach" the presenter, to make sure they are fully expressing the situation and their feelings about it. Then we, the listeners, ask questions to make sure we have a clear understanding of what the person is feeling. This helps us determine if we've experienced a time in our own life when we felt the same way. If we have, we share that story in the hope that it will be helpful.

But let's be real. When you present a situation to a room full of entrepreneurs, most people's first instinct is far from taking the Gestalt approach. Entrepreneurs, and leaders in general, have a tendency to feel like they're always having to fix something. That's what makes these forums so valuable.

We're forced to focus on sharing experiences rather than fixing problems. In fact, we actually have a "Gestalt only" card (think of a red card in soccer). When someone starts giving advice instead of sharing experiences, they get carded. When this happens, it reminds all of us that it's not our job to fix everything. People are capable of handling their own problems.

The most magical moments of the forum occur when everyone stays in Gestalt mindset. It's very affirming when people you respect connect with your experience by sharing similar situations from their own lives. It makes you feel like you aren't alone. Others have been there and survived. It gives you confidence that you have the tools to be successful—and that feeling unsure is just part of the experience.

This is the key to Understanding—the second pillar of the Approachable Leadership model. The way you create the Right Feeling is by seeking understanding. Do your best to create your own "forum" experience with those you lead.

 ## TOOL: Active Listening

Without the skill of active listening there is no way to achieve understanding. This tool provides practical tips on how to improve your active listening skills.

Right Feeling is created by a set of actions. We create the environment for listening and understanding when we:
- Pay attention
- Listen well
- Offer feedback
- Avoid judgment
- Respond (rather than Ignore)

Pay Attention
- Making eye contact
- Not thinking about your response

Listen well
- Nonverbal signs and cues—nod; lean-in
- Verbal cues—encourage, build, clarify, validate
- Use active listening phrases such as:
- Can you tell me more?
- What does that look like?
- I thought I heard you say...right?
- You seem [emotion] about this...
- What I hear you saying is...
- Have you considered...
- When you talk about this I notice [behavior]...
- You've obviously put a lot of effort into this...
- Let me make sure I understand you...
- Please tell me more about that...
- That sounds like a great story, tell me more...
- Is there anything else?

Offer feedback
Restate, reflect, summarize

Avoid judgment
Encourage, validate

Respond appropriately (don't ignore)
Restate, validate, reflect

Empathy Versus Sympathy: When Empathy Can Backfire

Creating understanding is harder than creating the Right Space. These conversations are deeper and more emotional than a first-level conversation focused on being open or welcoming. They're not superficial at all which means sometimes, because of that, they can be messy.

A number of behaviors help leaders create connections with understanding, but none is more important than empathy.

Despite what some people think, empathy is very different from sympathy.

Sympathy is about feeling *for* another person. And while sympathy does show that you care or are concerned, it also highlights that there is a difference between you and that person. And due to the nature of sympathy, often that difference is that you're better off than they are. As you can imagine, this increases distance.

Empathy, on the other hand, is about feeling *with* someone. In order to do this, you have to be able to recognize and share in the emotions of another person. This involves viewing the situation through their perspective, rather than yours. Empathy brings people closer. It implies that we are all equal.

Empathy Is Hard to Get Right

Being empathetic is hard, especially when you find yourself unable to relate to someone's situation. John Steinbeck captured this when he said,

> *"It means very little to know that a million Chinese are starving unless you know one Chinese who is starving."*

On the flip side of the coin, recent research by the *Harvard Business Review* found that,

> *"It's harder to empathize with people if you've been in their shoes."*

HBR gave two reasons for this.

First, people generally have difficulty accurately recalling just how difficult a past aversive experience was. Though we may remember that a past experience was painful, stressful, or emotionally trying, we tend to underestimate just how painful that experience felt in the moment. This phenomenon is called an "empathy gap."

Second, people who have previously overcome an aversive experience know that they were able to successfully overcome it, which makes them feel especially confident about their understanding of just how difficult the situation is.

The combined presence of "I can't recall how difficult it was" and "I know that I got through it myself" creates the perception that the event can be readily conquered, reducing empathy toward those currently struggling with a similar event.

Think about how this relates to approachability. A big part of being approachable is shrinking the "power distance gap" between you and your coworker. This "I've walked in your shoes" conversation increases distance instead of shrinking it. The person expressing frustration is likely to feel misunderstood or believe you think they are thin-skinned.

When an employee comes to us with an issue—whether it be personal or professional—we try to relate it to our own past experiences. This is natural and at least starts us in the right direction, but it's when we stop here, as the *HBR* research shows, that empathy backfires.

Rather than focusing on past *experiences*, we should focus on past *feelings*. Don't try to give their story a happy ending, just share about when you've felt a similar feeling. Sit in that uncomfortable place for a time. That is true empathy.

Theresa Wiseman, a nursing scholar, provided these four qualities of empathy in her often cited 1996 article *A Concept Analysis of Empathy*:

1. Perspective-taking, or the ability to take the perspective of another person (or recognizing that their perspective is their truth);

2. Staying out of judgment;
3. Recognizing emotion in other people; and
4. Communicating that emotional recognition.

Notice none of those steps is trying to make the other person feel anything other than what they are already feeling in that moment. They are all about being present. It's okay to recall walking a similar path before. But don't be in a hurry to tell where that path ultimately led for you. After all, your path was your path.

If you want to shrink power distance, just stand right there with the other person wherever they happen to be on their path. Then walk that path together.

 ## Lessons in Leadership: Freckles

An elderly woman and her little grandson, whose face was sprinkled with bright freckles, spent the day at the zoo. Lots of children were waiting in line to get their cheeks painted by a local artist who was decorating them with tiger paws.

"You've got so many freckles, there's no place to paint!" a girl in the line said to the little fella.

Embarrassed, the little boy dropped his head. His grandmother knelt down next to him. "I love your freckles. When I was a little girl I always wanted freckles," she said, while tracing her finger across the child's cheek.

"Freckles are beautiful." The boy looked up, "Really?"

"Of course," said the grandmother. "Why just name me one thing that's prettier than freckles."

The little boy thought for a moment, peered intensely into his grandma's face and softly whispered, "Wrinkles."

Teaching Empathy

Empathy isn't easy to teach. Some of us are naturally empathic, but many of us are not. It is the softest of "soft" skills. It can be easy to get it wrong even when you're trying. But it is the fundamental skill for creating the Right Feeling, a cornerstone of the Approachable Leadership model.

Like the boy in the story, empathy is expressed when you show *you understand how someone feels*. The boy realizes that his grandma feels the same way about her wrinkles as he does his freckles. He created the Right Feeling.

Many leaders blow the chance to create the Right Feeling because they immediately go into "fix it" mode. Sometimes they even cut off an employee as they're trying to explain the situation.

Do you ever react like this? Obviously, this kind of behavior is not approachable. Think about what you're really telling someone when you react this way. It tells the employee that:
- You think they are overreacting, weak, or somehow have a flawed view of their situation;

- They are bothering you and you don't have time to give them your full attention or to listen to their concern;
- Their problem is easy to solve and no big deal—they may even feel stupid for bringing it up (and discouraged from bringing up other problems in the future).

It may not be your intention, but it is what you're saying. And even if you do come up with a reasonable solution to their problem, you still kind of made them feel worse about it. This makes it less likely they'll approach you in the future.

So how do you change your tendencies? Start looking out for them. If you want to be more empathetic, more approachable, you have to catch yourself before you go into "fix it" mode. For that, we're going to turn to the SLC+C formula.

Stop. Listen. Confirm: Problem-Focused vs. Solution-Focused Questions

SLC stands for *Stop*, *Listen* and *Confirm*. Once you've done those three, you determine if it's right to add another C—*Collaborate on a solution*.

Let's look at each step.

Stop. The first step is stop. That's easy to say, but often hard to do. Stop means to put down your phone, turn away from your computer, and set aside any other distraction. Come to a complete, full stop.

Listen. Really listen to what this person has to say. Don't try to figure out what you're going to say next. Use active listening skills to make sure they feel that you're fully listening. Really focus on understanding what the other person is trying to communicate.

Confirm. The third step is to confirm understanding. Once this individual is finished explaining their situation and you feel like you understand it, try using this simple response: "You feel [emotion] because of [situation]. Do I have that right?"

At times, you may find yourself wanting to share an experience when you felt the same way. This is a good way to show empathy. However, remember the tips on empathy above. Be careful that you don't look like you're trying to "one up" the other person. *Never* say you know how they feel. Instead, share an experience that reminds you of a time you felt the way you think they feel now.

+ Collaborate. Avoid the temptation to give advice during these conversations. Only give advice when you are asked to do so. Even if you are asked to give advice you should be reluctant to provide it. Remember the Gestalt mindset. It is much more valuable for you to share your own experience, especially the feelings you had during that experience.

 **Tool: Empathy SLC+C Tool**

Empathy is hard. Leaders often feel like they need to have all the answers or they'll be seen as weak. Use this tool to help build your empathy skills and grow relationships.

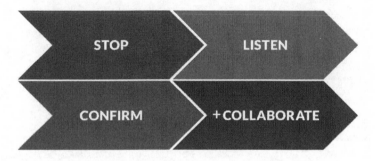

Stop. Give your attention, full stop.
- Put away your phone, close your laptop.
- Remove any distractions.
- If you can't pay attention, reschedule.
- Block uninterrupted time to meet.
- Close your door—ask for privacy.

Listen. Use active listening skills.
- Show speaker you are listening.
- Provide feedback (summarize, reflect).
- No judgment, encourage more.
- Respond appropriately (validate, restate).
- Focus on them—not what you will say next.

Confirm. Make sure you understand the situation and the feeling.

- "You feel _____ because of _____. Do I have that right?"
- Give them space to correct your interpretation.
- Remain in Gestalt mindset—don't give answers or advice.
- Sit with that feeling you just described, think about a time you felt the same way.
- Make sure you have confirmed understanding before moving to the next step.

Collaborate. If you are asked, use solution-focused questions to find an answer.

Avoid problem-focused questions.

- What's wrong?
- Why do you have this problem?
- Whose fault is it?
- How long has this been going on?
- What is this costing you?
- Why haven't you overcome this problem?

Ask solution-focused ones instead.

- What result do we really want?
- When can we start?
- What do we need to get started?
- What resources are available?

- Who can help?
- What can we start now?

Change Your Assumptions

Don't you just love it when someone who has just learned a tiny bit about your situation starts "helpfully" telling you what to do about it? Here is a quick leadership tip: Don't be *that* guy or gal.

Even the best intentioned advice can be demeaning. When you tell someone what to do, especially in a situation that is difficult or unclear, you are replacing their judgment with your own. You are basically saying you are smarter and more capable than them. If your advice is quick and assertive (the way many of us feel leaders are supposed to act), you have basically said their problem is simple to fix and they were dumb for not fixing it themselves.

Instead, if your assumption is that they can deal with this situation capably on their own, you approach the conversation in a very different way. Since your assumption is that they can come up with their own best solution, your job is simply to help them get to that point. It's more of a coaching conversation. You are just creating the Right Space and opportunity for them to think through and decide their own course of action.

You can certainly be a resource for that discussion. Part of that resource can be sharing your own experience under similar circumstances. But your goal is for them to come to their own conclusion and solution. This is good for two reasons.

1. They are way more likely to act on that decision.
2. You are building them up instead of acting as though your judgment is better than theirs.

A great tool for conversations like these are *solution-focused questions*. Solution-focused questions guide the discussion in a way that allows that person struggling with a problem to figure out the best solution for himself. This is in contrast to *problem-focused questions.*

Take a look at the two lists of questions from the bottom of the *Empathy Tool*. What do you notice about the problem-focused questions?

As the name implies, these statements relate to the problem that the person is facing. They are focused in the past and are mostly centered around blame. They also sound like an attempt by the advice-giver (leader) to ensure that he or she is not being blamed for the problem. They're accusatory. These questions create defensive, unproductive conversations.

Contrast that with the solution-focused questions.

These questions are focused on the future. Their assumption is one of abundance and many resources. The focus is on how *we* can solve this particular issue. The assumption is that we can solve it together.

There's one other big difference.

Problem-focused questions put you on the opposite side of the table from me. Solution-focused questions, however, have us sitting on the same side of the table.

Having said that, don't forget that you only pull out your solution-focused questions when you've been asked for advice. Collaboration is the last step and should only happen if the employee agrees that you understand the situation and you both agree to collaborate on a solution together.

Hello, Please, Thank You

Empathy isn't easy. It takes practice. If ever your attempts to be empathetic start feeling a little forced or overly complicated, just remember the point of empathy – to create the Right Feeling. And the most natural way to create the Right Feeling is to treat people with courtesy.

There are four "magic words" that can easily make you more approachable. They are:

Hello. Please. Thank you.

Yeah, I know. Your mom taught you that. Listen to your mom.

YOUR TURN ▶ Are you naturally good at empathy or is it a struggle? The next time someone approaches you with a challenge, practice responding with the SLC+C model.

Have you ever told someone about a problem only to have them immediately tell you that it's no big deal, or worse, fire off a solution before you've even finished explaining the situation? How did it make you feel?

Here are five ways to flex your empathy muscle:

1. Read, especially fiction.
2. Cultivate curiosity about strangers.
3. Ask questions.
4. Share vulnerably.
5. Diversify your social circle.

Review the *Active Listening Tool* and the *Empathy SLC+C Tool* before your next one-on-one meeting. Tell others you are working on your listening skills and ask for feedback. Do they notice?

CHAPTER 4

Follow Up and Follow Through: Support and "Right Action"

> If your actions inspire others to dream more, learn more, do more and become more, you are a leader.
>
> —John Quincy Adams

You have to walk the talk.

You can fake approachability for a while. You can be welcoming and have great conversations and be seen as approachable without really having to follow up or follow through with your employees. Many leaders fall into this category.

But over time, lack of follow-up and follow-through creates disappointment and leads your employees to feel that they can't rely on you. You have to prove through your actions that you are receptive to employee feedback and ideas. You have to take action. Otherwise you just push employees away.

Virtually every management training I've ever seen stresses the importance of follow-up and follow-through; but surprisingly, there is little good advice out there about how to do it.

The Habit of "Right Action"

Approachable Leaders are good at providing Support. Even leaders with the best intentions stumble on this third and last pillar of Approachable Leadership. Real engagement is about follow-through—taking what you learn from creating the right space and right feeling and putting it to work through Right Action.

Action speaks louder than words. This is what validates the rest of the conversation. Lack of follow-through destroys any credibility you build in the first two pillars.

A 2012 study in the *Journal of Business Ethics* calls this a "pseudo voice" problem. Pseudo voice refers to a leader who asks what you think but then doesn't do anything with whatever they learn. This behavior destroys trust and credibility. Specifically, the study found that:

> *...negative consequences are particularly likely to occur when employees perceive the opportunity to voice opinions to be "pseudo voice"—voice opportunity given by managers who do not have the intention to actually consider employee input (i.e. managerial disregard).*

The researchers found that employees of "pseudo voice" managers are 61% less likely to give feedback in their organization. More troubling, employees of these leaders are 65% more likely to have conflict with coworkers.

On the flip side, the researchers found that the positive effects of following through on employee suggestions include: increased feelings of fairness, trust, decision control, inclusion in the group, and respect.

When done right, you can have these kinds of results too. However, Right Action, like most things, is easier said than done. It's a positive habit that comes about through consistency and practice.

Here's a few practical tips to get you started on the right path.

 ## Tool: Follow-Up Rules and Tools

One of the top takeaways attendees of our Approachable Leadership Workshop always mention is our exercise on *Follow-Up and Follow-Through Rules and Tools*. We start by looking over the diagram on the next page:

Next, each person lists at least one Follow-Up Rule and one Follow-Up Tool that fits into one of the six areas.

A *Follow-Up Rule* comes from your personal standard operating procedure. It is a commitment you make to yourself and others about how you will handle certain situations. Your rule can focus inward or outward. For example, an outward-focused rule might be that you return all phone calls within four hours, or that you return emails within 24 hours. An inward-focused rule might be to take action on anything that you can finish in less than two minutes.

A *Follow-Up Tool* is something that helps you keep your commitments to take action. This includes things like your calendar, to-do list, in-box, phone, email, text messaging apps, etc. It also includes your processes, like how you schedule meetings. Tools can be virtual, such as reminders or organization apps on your phone or computer. Or they can be physical. A lot of people swear by good old pen and paper (that's where I keep my daily to-do list and notes).

The reason this exercise is my favorite is because follow-up and follow-through is the area I personally struggle with most as a leader, and I have learned a lot from other leaders and experts through this exercise.

Read through the examples and recommendations below and pick one to try over the next week. If it works, keep it in your routine. Either way, pick another one from another area the next week. Continue trying out rules and tools that you think can improve your follow-up and follow-through. But be careful not to add something just because it's on the list. Keep your system useful *for you*.

Simple Rules and Tools for Follow-Up and Follow-Through

Below is a brief description of the six areas in the *Follow-Up and Follow-Through Tool*, as well as some good rules and tools I have received from successful leaders over the years.

Hopefully some of these will help you develop your own follow-up rules and tools.

1. Create an Action-Friendly Environment

Today we live in an "always on" world, one where we are constantly bombarded and interrupted. Effective leaders have to manage their attention and focus. You have to create an environment that supports follow-up and follow-through.

The best way to do that is to set up your environment to support taking action. A number of the ideas below will help you do this.

First, think about all the things in your current environment that distract you from follow-up or follow-through. Once you have done this, use this knowledge to develop rules and tools to create a more supportive environment.

2. Use an Accountability Partner, Co-Mentor, or Coach

Follow-up and follow-through isn't sexy. It can be tedious and boring. Some of us are more likely to actually get something done if we have someone to help us along.

That's where the idea of an accountability partner comes in. Accountability partners give you someone to talk to about your experience. You can celebrate a success or discuss a struggle. The most important thing is that you have support system. It also creates an incentive to actually do the exercise. No one wants to let their partner down.

Maybe even make follow-up a contest or game. Or embrace guilt trips (some of us need that kind of a nudge). Whatever it takes to get you and your accountability partner out there taking action.

3. Schedule It

Do you ever go through a day and realize you didn't look at your to-do list once? Me too.

Another habit for good follow-through is using your calendar. Planning doesn't have to be a quarterly or annual thing. Planning can be a daily and weekly habit that can give you more buffer time and sense of control over your time.

Most of us look at our calendar several times each day (even if it is just to triple check that we really don't have back-to-back meetings scheduled all day). When you commit to doing something, block time for it right then. This accomplishes two things:

First, if you schedule time to act on items—and are honest with yourself about how long they will take—you can visually see when you are overcommitting.

Second, once something is scheduled you are much more likely to do it. At the very least you'll have a reminder there, with time set aside for doing it. If life gets in the way, move the time block. Still, you are much less likely to forget about it if it's staring you in the face.

4. Establish Simple, Concrete, Actionable Rules

Tools are great, but your habits and your discipline are more important. One of the most effective things you can do to be good at follow-through is to establish default rules and procedures that help you make it happen in the moment.

For example, commit to answer calls and emails within a certain period of time. Or charge yourself with writing down any follow-up item in your journal as it happens. Require yourself to end every meeting by summarizing next actions. This way, everyone agrees on and understands what is going to happen next.

In the Your Turn section at the end of this chapter, I've listed a number of rules and tools to get you started. Think about what guidelines you want to set for yourself.

 ## Lessons in Leadership: Chasing Shiny Objects

I have a tendency to chase shiny objects, especially if those shiny objects happen to come in the form of productivity apps and systems. I like to read productivity books and blogs and listen to productivity podcasts. I want to make sure I'm not missing the latest technological solution that magically solves all my follow-through concerns.

The lesson in this is that if you added up all the time I've spent over the years playing around with new productivity tools and systems, I could probably have written two or three more books...

Which is precisely why, these days, I'm spending less and less time downloading new productivity apps. I'm focusing instead on productivity rules and habits.

Still, I am far from the poster child for follow-up and follow-through (if you send me a non-urgent email it is not unheard of for me to reply a month later–sorry!) but I'm working on it. And I hope you do too.

5. Just Start...and Build Momentum

Let me play Captain Obvious for a second. Follow-up and follow-through starts with *action*. Approachable Leaders move the ball forward on every play.

Teddy Roosevelt famously said:

> *"In any moment of decision, the best thing you can do is the right thing, the next best thing is the wrong thing, and the worst thing you can do is nothing."*

You can have the best system and process in the world. List out all your next actions along with their proper context. Get all your to-do items placed in A-B-C priority. But until you move, you've accomplished exactly nothing.

I am not suggesting that beginning with the end in mind, prioritizing, planning, and delegating aren't all vital leadership skills. But the one that's most often missing is action.

Something magical happens when you start moving items from the "to-do" list to the "done" list. You get momentum. One item begets the next. Your coworkers will start to see you as more reliable and someone they can count on to get stuff done. This is how you build real credibility as a leader with your staff, your peers and your own leaders.

Still, it's important to remember that movement for the sake of moving isn't without its problems. You have to look up every so often—it's the only way to confirm that your movement is productive and you're going the direction you want to go.

Even taking into account the roadblocks, I think Teddy's advice is right on. Move the right direction if you can. And moving the wrong direction is still a lot better than doing nothing.

At least your employees see that you're trying (and, on that note, that you're human).

6. Make It Habit and Routine

A great way to make sure you keep moving forward is to make follow-up and follow-through a habit and part of your routine. Think about each of the areas listed above. Are there ways you can build them into your daily and weekly routine? Can you make them a natural part of the way you go through your day? Can you make room on your schedule for certain activities—such as standing staff and 1-on-1 meeting agendas or routines for approving expenses, signing agreements, and other actions that are crucial to keeping the ball moving for yourself and your reports?

Habit formation takes effort, especially if the habits you have now distract you from good follow-through. Charles Duhigg wrote brilliantly on the subject in his book *The Power of Habit*.

The core principle in Duhigg's book is that habits form when *cues* send us into a *routine*. That routine gives us some sort of *reward*. This loop is repeated again and again and becomes a habit.

For example, what is the first thing do when you sit down at your desk to wake up your computer? If you are like most people, you either open up your email or a social media page like Facebook or LinkedIn.

Sitting down and waking up your computer is a *cue*. That *cue* starts the *routine* of opening up your email or social media page. You get the *reward* of a dopamine dump when you check your email or social media notifications. In fact, companies like Facebook and LinkedIn spend a ton of money making sure that's exactly what happens when you visit. That reward means you'll be returning again soon.

How can you make the habit of follow-up or follow-through part of that routine? Duhigg suggests changing one of the three elements of the habit—the cue, routine, or the reward. In this case the cue is sitting down at your desk, so the best thing to look at is the routine.

What if every time you sat at your desk you first pulled out your to-do list, completed one action, and checked one item off the list? Your reward for checking off the to-do item would be visiting your email or your Facebook page. Now you have hacked the habit routine to include follow-up or follow-through.

This is just one example. You probably have a dozen or more routines during your normal workday. Can you think of other ways to incorporate follow-up or follow-through into those routines? Start incorporating them and it won't take long before you can turn yourself into a follow-through ninja.

In the end, your goal is to make follow-up and follow-through part of your identity as a leader. You don't do it to mark something off a list or because it is something you're supposed to do. You do it because it is who you are.

 **YOUR TURN**

Here are some rules and tools that can help you become a follow-up and follow-through ninja.

Follow-Up Rules to Experiment with:
- Clean up your workspace each day before you leave.
- List your top three to-do items for the next day before you leave.
- Empty your in-boxes (physical and virtual) each day and add follow-up items to your to-do list.
- Limit your in-boxes (ideally to one physical and one virtual in-box).
- Don't turn on your computer or tablet until you have taken a walk through the work area.
- Only check email at certain times each day.
- Arrive at work 30 minutes before your team to prepare for the day.
- Make follow-up an agenda item for all meetings.
- Follow through on one to-do item before you wake up your computer each time you sit at your desk.
- Add follow-up to your morning or evening routine.
- Commit to send out a weekly follow-up communication that contains all follow-up from that week.
- Hold a weekly meeting where follow-up items are closed or updated.
- Add follow-up and in-box opportunities to your daily startup meeting agenda.
- Turn off your phone (airplane mode works in areas other than airplanes!) or computer and spend time focusing on follow-up.

- Never leave your desk without your tools (note cards, notebook, phone, etc.)—always have an in-box and follow-up list close at hand.

Add your favorite Follow-Up Rules:

_____

_____

_____

Supportive Environment Tools to Experiment with:
- Use an obvious, physical in-box where people know they can put items they want you to see.
- Use an "Always Around" in-box where you can capture follow-up items (a notebook, notecards, or a phone app are the most common).
- Some people like to use a "dictation" app so to-do items can be captured by voice (for example Siri can add items to your reminders list or a document by just speaking them into your phone).
- Consider using a "location-aware" to-do app, that can remind you to take an action when you are in a certain location (like picking up a form when you are at the corporate office).
- Use a whiteboard or other obvious place to put your key to-do items, follow-up items, or issue-tracking system.
- Share an Excel® spreadsheet or other electronic board with your team so they can see progress on open items or when items are closed.
- Set a calendar event or alarm to look at your to-do list or follow-up list two or three times a day–it is

easy to get distracted and this is a good way to bring attention back to your list.

- Look at a Pomodoro timer—this can be as simple as setting a timer on your phone or as elaborate as apps that shut off selected phone apps or websites for a set period of time (usually 25 minutes at a time) so you can focus on single-tasking or getting things done.
- Block time in your calendar for follow-up activities, agenda planning for the next day, and for focused time.

Add your favorite Supportive Environment Tools:

_____

_____

_____

CHAPTER 5

Monday Morning Approachability: Creating Right Space, Right Feeling, and Right Action Every Day

> " *Successful people are simply those with successful habits.* "
>
> —Brian Tracy

You are convinced. You are committed to being a more approachable leader. You're excited and you're ready to rock. And then...you hit the real world.

You don't have time. You're stressed. So are your people. You haven't been the most approachable leader in the past but, full of newbie enthusiasm, you jump out on that limb and you ask someone, "What would make work better?"

First, they look at you like you grew a new head. Then, they realize you're not joking. A slight smile crosses their face. Then, boom—they let you have it. You are overwhelmed with all the pent-up frustrations, wouldas, and couldas. You want to head to happy hour, and it's only 10am. Or, you spend a week taking small steps, just as I've suggested, and it's taking a ton of your mental energy and you just don't see the use.

Continuing the Journey: Dealing with Roadblocks

The vast majority of your employees will be pleasantly surprised as you try being more approachable. Many will notice and may even compliment you. You should assume that's how people will respond. But some won't.

Some employees will give you a hard time. You may even deserve it. Perhaps you haven't been the most approachable leader recently. It happens. Some employees are so invested in fighting with the boss that they may make a show out of mocking your new behavior.

What can you do when faced with this situation? First, it is extremely important not to react in the moment. That's going to be hard, but it's important. Reflect on what's happening. Any time you try out a new skill or behavior, you should expect challenges. It won't be natural to you or anyone else.

Most people really just don't like change. It's uncomfortable and resistance is natural. Even if the change is seen as a move in the right direction, the natural reaction is to fall back into old habits.

Use this to your advantage. Expect obstacles and pushback. This gives you an opportunity to plan for a response. Think about the kinds of things people might say in a worst case scenario. Practice dealing with them with your accountability partner. (You identified someone while working through the

Follow-Up and Follow-Through exercises, right?) For example:

> *What, have you been reading some psycho-babble management book? What's with all the questions?*

> *You lost? I haven't seen you out of your office this much ever.*

> *I'd really love to talk to you, but somebody has to work around here and that somebody is me.*

How might you respond to statements like these? What is the approachable reply to this kind of pushback?

First, assume positive intent. This person ultimately does want a better relationship and this reaction is a defense mechanism. With that as your assumption, now ask yourself why someone might behave this way. Can you think of any reasons? Walk a mile in their shoes.

What might be happening that would cause a reaction like this? Have you ever felt this way about a boss of yours? Do you understand how they're feeling? Remember what we learned about the SLC+C (stop, listen, confirm and collaborate) model.

If you assume positive intent, you are less likely to act defensively (or escalate the situation). Instead, you will respond with understanding. Here are some things that you could say to someone who notices your change in behavior (whether they give you positive feedback or a hard time). Consider a reply like:

I'm really glad you've noticed. This is something that I'm working on and I'm glad that it's coming across.

I know you're frustrated and I haven't always been the best to work with. It's something I'm trying to work on. I hope that you'll be patient with me and that you'll give me a chance to be better.

Keep me honest. I need your feedback and I want to hear from you. If you feel like things are slipping, please let me know.

It's a good idea to pair up with a partner, co-mentor, or coach (many HR departments are beginning to provide these leadership development opportunities with internal and external staff) and practice how you might deal with situations like these. Practice responding to someone who gives you positive feedback. Get a feel for what that's like. Next, respond to somebody who gives you negative feedback. Practice these conversations until you feel comfortable.

Remember, this journey won't be a straight line. It's more like climbing a rock wall. You want to get comfortable with your hand hold and your footing in one spot, and then stretch to reach the next level. It may be a jagged path. You may feel like you are hanging in one place or on a plateau. Other times you may feel like you're making quick progress.

Don't worry about the destination. Focus on the journey. Add these new behaviors and new tools to your toolbox and then occasionally take a look back and see how far you've come. I bet you'll surprise yourself.

 ### Lessons in Leadership:
Sometimes You Have to Get Creative

What if you can't deliver what someone wants or needs? No matter how much you care or desire to help, sometimes you can't. You don't have the power or the resources. This is especially true for new leaders.

Many supervisors I meet feel frustrated and powerless to take action or influence things in their organization. This does not have to be a barrier to Approachable Leadership if you are up-front and authentic with those you lead. Explain what you can influence and what you can't.

The best way to do this? Focus on the relationship and making progress.

I recently worked with an assembly line/operations supervisor named Brian in a manufacturing facility. Brian was frustrated. His "go-to" guy, Tony, wanted to train on a different operation in the Quality Control department. Brian mentioned it to the QC lead a couple of times and was getting nowhere. He felt powerless. Not only that, but Tony was getting upset too. Brian asked if I could think of anything to help.

"What can you control here?" I asked Brian. "Nothing, that's the problem," Brian grumbled.

"Oh, come on, you are a rising star here," I replied. "Your name comes up all the time when talk turns to potential leaders—surely you can come up with something!"

We started a list of some things he could influence. It was slow going at first, but eventually he listed a few items.

As we worked through the list, Brian's body language and attitude transformed. He grew confident. He felt like he could help Tony after all. Then, Brian suggested an idea that stood out among all the rest.

"Tony and I could come up with an idea or two in our department that could apply in Quality."

Brian and Tony came up with a great efficiency idea. They knew it would work better in Quality than it did in Assembly. They tried it for a month in Assembly and tracked the progress.

Tony put together some impressive charts that proved the new process was saving hours each month while simultaneously reducing re-work.

Together, he and Brian presented the results during the monthly lean meeting. The leader of the Quality department had several good questions and it was obvious she immediately saw where the process would work in her department. After the meeting, she came up and talked to Tony a little more.

She sheepishly asked Brian, "Is it cool if Tony helps us implement this in our department for a month?" Brian, trying hard not to be too snarky, said it was cool. He and Tony high-fived each other later.

Focusing on things you can't effectively influence is frustrating and demotivating. Focusing instead on things you can influence is energizing and gets you moving. Thinking about next steps completely changes your point of view and your view of what's possible. The next time you're stuck, just think about the next step to get the ball rolling. That might be the only nudge you need to end up in a place that at first seemed impossibly far away.

Leading Through Limited Control and Uncertainty

If someone asks about something beyond your span of control, take a few lessons from Brian. First, be clear about what you can and can't influence.

Most leaders hate to admit we can't make something happen. But leaving the impression you'll fix something when you can't sets you up for a big fall. You not only fail in your attempt to follow through with Right Action, but you also miss a big opportunity to create Right Feeling.

Why? Because times like this demand resourcefulness, and working together on a challenge builds understanding and connection. When you are up front about your limitations, you become vulnerable. You and the person you lead are faced with the same challenge. It gives you a great opportunity to dig into why this person desires the change.

What would meet her needs? How would it impact her life at work or outside of work? Do these needs make sense? Are there other ways to meet them?

These are powerful conversations that build a bridge to understanding. And they start when you reveal your own frustrations and challenges.

One important caution: Resist the temptation to "throw your company under the bus" by saying you disagree with a business decision. Most business decisions are made for valid reasons. Also, companies don't want to do wrong by valuable team members. Always attempt to understand the business reasons for a decision.

If you don't understand a decision, respectfully try to figure it out. Sometimes your own efforts to understand can help a company realize a flaw or improve on an idea. Either way, you will be in a much better position to explain the decision to your team.

This is especially important when you, personally, understand the decision, but you still disagree with it.

My friend Max Dubroff has a great rule of thumb for these occasions:

"Never complain down or to the side; only complain up."

Complaining right along with your employees isn't going to solve anything, even if you agree with them. In fact, it will likely add fuel to the fire. The best action you can take as a leader is to clarify the reasons behind the decision, answer any questions, and empathize if the change creates frustration. Then make sure your coworkers have the resources they need, and get out of the way.

Create the open and welcoming Right Space where employees feel comfortable coming to you with questions, concerns, or just to chat. When approached, make sure you fully understand and connect. Finally, when needed, agree to take action and follow through. Make people feel wanted and understood and do your best to be a good neighbor and help others make progress in their lives.

You will see your relationships strengthen, results improve, and your own leadership grow.

The Case for Approachability

I began this book describing how we've watched leaders battle through their toughest situations. Some succeeded. Many failed. Over the years we've watched these leaders carefully and identified a number of simple habits that separated the successful ones from the rest. Over and over, we discovered that the thing that separated the successful leaders from those who did not fare as well was their approachability.

If you've read this far, you must now believe approachability can improve your leadership. And you're probably realizing that this involves a lot more than some "soft skill" that's "nice to have." New research shows that approachability delivers real business results in areas like:
- Cooperation
- Enthusiasm
- Employee commitment
- Workplace stress

According to a 2015 study from the University of Tulsa (that we helped with), employees who rate their supervisor "approachable" are *89% more likely to report satisfaction with their work*. They also note better relationships with coworkers.

89%

Employees of Approachable Leaders are happy and less stressed at work

Source: University of Tulsa, 2015

Plus, employees of approachable leaders are *more willing to go "above and beyond" at work*. They are 88% more likely to make suggestions or volunteer to pitch in outside their normal job. Behaviors like these improve cooperation, drive innovation and deliver business results.

88%

Approachability predicts "above and beyond" behavior more than all other factors

Source: Journal of Management Development, 2005

Another surprising finding was that *approachability trumps other leader competencies*. Nearly 10% of the employees in this study had a low opinion of their supervisor. They went "above and beyond" anyway. The difference between these folks and those who let their frustration keep them on the sideline?

People who like their manager and are enthusiastic about their work don't quit.

These employees still felt their leader was approachable. It's that simple. That's why it's not surprising that the more approachable you are, the less likely your employees will consider leaving.

Employees of Approachable Leaders do not intend to quit their jobs

Source: University of Tulsa, 2015

Turnover wastes precious time, money, and energy. It frustrates everyone who has to pick up the slack (especially your high performers, who you can least afford to lose). Approachable leaders put a stop to that negative cycle.

This is just one of the studies cited in The Playbook. For more, see http://approachableleadership.com/research.

Approachability Is Teachable

There are thousands of things you can teach leaders. Trustworthiness and charisma (to name just two) are well-researched leader behaviors associated with positive business results.

No question these behaviors are desirable. But they are hard to affect through training. How do you reliably train someone to be more trustworthy? Or more charismatic?

Training "soft skill" basics (dealing with team dysfunction, conversation skills) is very useful, but often fails to get at the fundamental behaviors that reinforce strong leader relationships.

Approachable Leadership can solve this problem. It is simpler to learn, accessible, quickly understood, and easy to observe and practice. This makes it the **ideal habit for leaders to develop**.

Help Spread the Word about Approachable Leadership

Would you help us spread the word about Approachable Leadership? Here are four things you can do now:

1. **Share approachability.** Know someone who would enjoy the book? All you have to do is go to http://ALplaybook.com and fill out the "share the book" form. We will send a copy (with your compliments) to them. *What's more approachable than that?*

2. **Join the conversation.** Let your network know about the Playbook and your approachability journey in the comments at http://ALplaybook.com or on LinkedIn, Facebook or Twitter. Anything you can do to spread the word is greatly appreciated. Use the hashtag #ApproachableLeadership so we can find your post and say thanks!

3. **Bring Approachable Leadership® to your company or community.** Whether you need a Keynote speaker for your next company training, industry or professional association event, or want to deliver our Workshop or Learning System to your leaders, we'd love to discuss the options. We customize our message for any group. Learn more at ApproachableLeadership.com/Speaking

4. **Have a voice. Tell us what you think.** We love to hear from students about how they've applied approachability in their lives. Let us know how it's helping you or if there's anything you think we can do to make this material more useful to your or your team. Experiencing challenges or roadblocks? Let us know. We also are happy to coach you through it. Please drop us a line or comment at http://ALplaybook.com

Thank you for joining us on this Approachable Leadership journey. We look forward to seeing you out there!

What's Your Next Play?

You've read the playbook. What's next?

Share *The Approachability Playbook*. Tell your friends and colleagues about *The Playbook*. Go to ALplaybook.com and use the sharing options to tell others how they can receive their own copy of *The Approachability Playbook*.

Download Your Free Tools. Go to ALplaybook.com where you can download FREE, ready-to-use templates of all the tools in *The Playbook*.

Take and Share the Quiz. Take the "Good Boss" quiz at ALplaybook.com then ask your co-workers, friends, family... and your boss to take it! You get a custom-tailored report highlighting specific actions you can take to build strong daily approachability habits into your routine.

Continue the Discussion. Join the discussion by comparing notes with your friends and colleagues (the discussion board is at the bottom of the page at ALplaybook.com) and continue the conversation about approachability. This will help keep the idea on the top of your mind while you are working to develop the habits.

About Approachable Leadership

At *Approachable Leadership* our mission is to help you tackle 3 major challenges facing businesses today:

- The *Cooperation Gap* (**3/4** of all change projects fail, and **53%** of those projects destroy value);
- the *Enthusiasm Gap* (**71%** of employees are disengaged, costing an estimated **$550 billion**); and
- the *Talent Gap* (**20%** of workers will voluntarily quit this year, costing businesses **$11 billion**).

These issues are stumbling blocks to success. Many companies mistakenly attack these challenges with a "whack-a-mole" approach that drains resources and energy.

How does Approachability address these challenges?

- Approachable leaders see **88% more "above and beyond" behavior** from their teams.
- Employees with Approachable leaders are **89% more likely to be engaged**.
- Turnover intention **decreases by 71%**.

The **Approachable Leadership Learning System** can replace or complement your current leader development strategy. Use our content with your current internal trainers (with support from our learning coaches) or bring our coaches to your company to implement the learning system.

Improve cooperation and enthusiasm. Keep your talent. **Call 800-888-9115 to learn about bringing a tailored Approachable Leadership solution to your company.**

About the Author

Phillip B. Wilson, is the founder of Approachable Leadership. He is a national expert on leadership, labor relations and creating positive workplaces. He is regularly featured in the business media including *Fox Business News*, *Fast Company*, *Bloomberg News*, *HR Magazine*, and *The New York Times*.

Wilson is a highly regarded speaker, trainer, and an adjunct professor. Phil delivers keynotes, workshops and webinars regularly for conferences, industry groups, and companies across North America and Canada.

Phil is the author of multiple books and publications. In addition to *The Approachability Playbook*, he authored *Left of Boom: Putting Proactive Engagement to Work* (which reached #2 on Amazon's Hot HR Books list). Other books and publications include: *The Next 52 Weeks, Managing the Union Shop, Model Contract Clauses*, among many others.

Phil has been called on multiple occasions to testify before Congress as a labor relations expert. He graduated magna cum laude from Augustana College in Rock Island, Illinois, and went on to earn his J.D. from the University of Michigan Law School.

Made in the USA
Charleston, SC
11 November 2016